MW01469799

# The Light, the Dark, and the In Between

*Stacy Kestwick*

*a poetry collection*

USA TODAY Bestselling Author
# STACY KESTWICK

Cover Design by Melissa Panio-Petersen
Illustrations by WMW
Edited by Erin Noelle
Formatting by Champagne Book Design

For anyone who has had their heart broken, reassembled the pieces, and found the remix to be even better.

a poetry collection

At the concert
Surrounded by people music lights
I sang along and danced
Next to you
We didn't touch once
That whole night
You never even noticed

It's amazing what you become used to
Slowly
Stealthily
Over time
All the little ways you're told you're
Not enough
Until your default answer to everything is
I'm sorry
It's my fault
I'm sorry
For being me
I'm sorry
I'm sorry
I'm sorry
Until one day
The only thing left to say is
I'm sorry
I can't stay
I'm sorry
I'm leaving

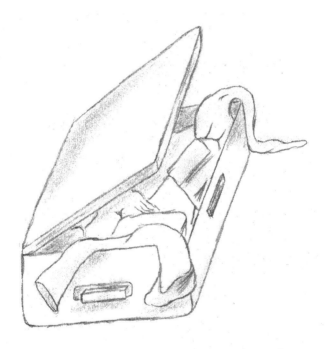

You play the victim so well
But I wonder who you'll blame now
That I'm no longer there
To be the villain

You made fidelity seem
Like an unreasonable request
A standard men simply cannot
Be expected to reach
Then acted shocked
When I raised my standards
To the height they should've been at all along
And you
No longer qualified

My mind has this bad habit
Of overthinking every little
Word and action and gesture
And twisting it around
To a negative connotation
I've broken my own heart
More times
Than you ever will

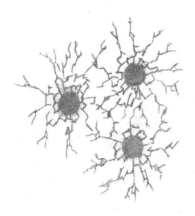

We met young
I thought we'd have one of those
Epic love stories
That grandchildren brag about
Opposites attract
And make a perfect whole
That can't be broken
Except
There were holes
And I tried to patch them
And look past them
And ignore when the same holes ripped open again
My attempts at repairing them
An utter failure
I learned
Eventually
The hard way
One half can't fix a hole
One half can't fix a whole

If the hardest lessons
Are disguised as
Our worst failures
Then congratulations
You were my best teacher

Don't be so surprised
That my words are intelligent
Just because my hair
Is pink

You liked to tell me
What I shouldn't do
What I shouldn't wear
Why I should step back
Why I should stay quiet
You wanted me to be less
So you could be more
I'm sorry
I scared you so much
I'm sorry
I was too much for you
But not sorry enough
To stay

You betrayed me
And I tried to convince myself
That was okay
We had history
Inside jokes
Small children
A mortgage
The same last name
It took me far too long to realize
Trust
Can't be replaced

There are far worse things
Than being alone
Like staying
Long after
You should've gone

You made me a woman
In a tomato field
In a tent beneath the summer sun
Stolen minutes beside a borrowed truck
After it was over
A butterfly appeared
And fluttered around us
Almost tame
I was enchanted
And then you said
It was the devil
Watching us
Judging us
And we were going to hell
Thanks, asshole

The worst is when
You can see all the subtle signs
The evasive answers
The broken eye contact
The lousy excuses
Pointing to inevitable heartbreak
And you're just waiting for
When and where
To turn into
Then and there

If I thought your

Words hurt,

It's only because I hadn't yet felt

The pain of your silence

I knew it was over

When an eternity alone

Sounded better than

One more day

With you

Those people that say

Love conquers all
Love never dies
All you need is love

Those people
Are full of shit

Because no amount of love
Can replace
Trust and respect
Once it's gone

It didn't matter how
I spread my legs
Bent my knees
Raised my ass
Opened my mouth
You were never satisfied
It didn't matter how
Fast I pumped
Slow I kissed
Soft I stroked
Long I lasted
You were never satisfied
It didn't matter
I was never the problem

How much of the blame
Falls on me
For forgiving you
When I should've
Just left

The night after I became a mother
You left
To check on the dog
Who was at home alone
I didn't realize that by dog
You meant some faceless woman
In a parking lot
Who was lonely in the back of her car

After years
You knew exactly which buttons to push
To hurt me
And you knew exactly when to do it
To inflict the most pain
Which vulnerabilities to pick at
To chip away at my self-confidence
You still fire those words like bullets
Trying to reach me
Trying to do damage from afar
What you don't understand
Is you'll never touch me
Ever again

I trusted
Far too easily
I trusted
Again and again
Long after I shouldn't have
Certain that this time
I'd be enough
That you'd really changed
That you meant all the pretty words you said
I forgave
Because people make mistakes
And maybe it really was all my fault
After all
I left
Far too late
After you broke my heart
Again and again
Because you didn't change
I wasn't enough
And all those pretty words
Were bullshit

It's true what they say

You can't make someone change their mind

If they aren't ready

Sometimes

You have to let people be their own downfall

I was always cold
You were always hot
But you were the man
And your comfort was
Obviously more important
So we always kept it cold
And I bundled up
Year round
In hoodies and extra socks
And blankets
And you complained that I didn't dress sexier
For you
When it felt like winter
Between us

I don't need you to
Plant doubt in my head
Sabotage my efforts
Put barriers in my path

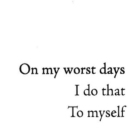

On my worst days
I do that
To myself

We were together for decades
Your family became mine
It was so much harder
Losing them
Than losing you

You taught me things

I wish I never

Had to learn

It's so hard
The day when your
Parents are no longer superheroes
And instead
Are merely
Human
When you leave your childhood behind
And stumble into adulthood
Navigating the best you can
Just like them

I'll give you this
You were dependable
You betrayed me
Again and again
And every time
You would apologize
And make empty promises
About how
This time
It would be different
And I wanted so bad to
Believe you
So bad for you to actually
Fucking mean it
But I guess bad habits
Are hard to break
Unlike my heart

It's shocking

That after years together

You became a stranger

So quickly

It makes me wonder

If I ever really knew you

At all

Somewhere along the way
I outgrew you
I became too much
And you kept trying to
Shove me back into the same box
I used to fit in
But I couldn't breathe in there
I was suffocating
Leaving was the only way
To survive

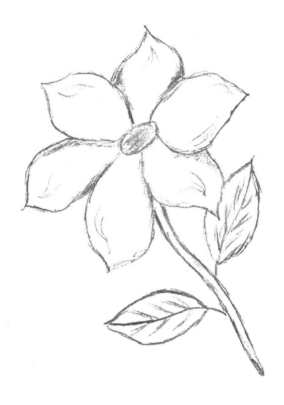

My biggest fear
    Is being inconsequential
        I want to matter
           To someone
                Who matters to me

Silence

Can cut deeper

Than the harshest words

Leaving behind

Invisible scars

That never heal

I don't understand
Your need to cling to
Pointless bitterness
Over us ending
There's no prize
For being miserable
Let go
Move forward
(I sure as hell did)

You claim you found Jesus
And you've redeemed yourself
Served your penance and
Found morality for the first time in your life
All I've seen is
A metamorphosis
From sinner to sanctimonious
Good luck with that

A little part of me
Since childhood
Has feared the dark
But what I've learned
Is the scariest monsters
Walk in the daylight
And don't bother with masks

I used to think
You were misunderstood
I was the only one
Who could see your charm
Because I was special
I saw the real you
The one you kept hidden
From everyone else
I used to be
An idiot

You blame me
For leaving you
And that's fine
Failing at something
Has never felt
So good

Divorce requires
The government's permission to fail at love
Requirements must be met
An official decree drawn up to
Verify the relationship's demise
An obituary for the heart
With time and cause of death
Pronounced by lawyers instead of doctors
Recorded for everyone to read
And printed in the newspapers so it can't be missed
It's a peculiar death
The end of a former identity
And way of life
Buried in black and white and the
Grim reality of
Shared custody and divided assets

                              You would think
                         There would at least
                                    Be cake

I thought I could fix us
With tenacity and time
But we were doomed
Without trust

Goodbye

Is one of the

Most painful words

Ever created

How sad to think
How easy it would've been
To have never met you
One of a million little things
Happening just slightly differently
And you and I
Would've never become
Us

No one to criticize
My career
My hair color
My thermostat setting
My cooking
My driving
My night owl tendencies
My hobbies
My clothes
My friends
My afternoon nap
My make-up
My body
My goals
My hopes
My dreams
My soul
I'm alone
But
Not lonely

The bed is so much bigger
Without you
And all the blame
You stacked around me
Like extra pillows
Just there for decoration
Just there to smother me

It's daunting
Starting again from scratch
Being alone doesn't scare me
But it's not my first choice
Will someone want a body
That's made two babies?
A mangled heart with
A tendency to expect the worst
And apologize for everything?
Will someone be patient with me
While I relearn to trust
And find my missing self-confidence?
Or have all the good ones
Been taken by
Younger
Prettier
More worthy girls?
Is anyone's first choice
The leftovers?

It would be easy to hate you
For everything that's happened
But we made two tiny humans
Who own my heart
And they're half me
But they're also
Half you

Some days
I'm my biggest fan
Some days
I'm my worst enemy
Some days
I just want the inner monologue
To shut the fuck up
And I crank the music
Extra loud
To drown myself out

I've learned

The difference between

A boy and a man

Is simple

Boys talk

Men act

It's easy
To get stuck
Playing a game
You know you're going to lose
Because
If nothing else
The game is familiar
Sometimes
The bravest thing you can do
Is admit defeat
And start over

The thing about the dark times
Is they don't stay dark forever
And if you can just keep moving forward
One day
Step
Inch
Breath
At a time
Eventually
You'll find the light again
And it'll shine even brighter than before

I don't miss the eggshells
I used to walk on around you
Now I crank the music
And dance in the kitchen
And scramble the fuck
Out of the eggs
Whenever I damn well please

I still apologize for everything
Even though you hate that
But some habits
Are hard to break
After so long
~~I'm sorry~~

Nothing is worse than when
Your heart and your brain
Disagree
When half of you has to lose
So the other half can win

Everything happens for a reason
Right?
That's what they say
And I used to wonder what the lesson was for me
When he cheated
Now I know
It was to discover my own strength
It was to learn my true worth
It was to demand better
It was to find you

The words come so much easier
At night
When the world is still and sleeping
And the voice in my head
Breaks the silence
And demands to be heard

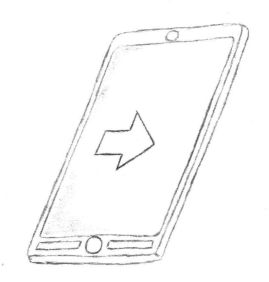

Modern dating
I swipe
Left
Right
A catalogue of men
I sort some into my shopping cart
To keep for later
To be tried on for size
I hope one fits

It's no wonder the ones
Who have been hurt the most
Love the hardest
The light is so much more beautiful
When you've been stuck in the dark
For too long

I've always found clarity
In the moonlight
The sun is too bright
Too dazzling
Too distracting
I prefer the night
When the world is
Quiet and sleeping
That's when the truth
Tiptoes out
And whispers in my ear

We might be over
But I got the best parts of you
So despite everything
Thank you for being in my life
Thank you for making me a mother

How do you know
When you're healed?
When you can smile again?
When the memory doesn't
Bring you pain?
Or when you reach a level
Of blessed apathy?

You're not the original version anymore
You broke along the way
Picked yourself up
Patched yourself together
Kept moving
And look at you now
The sequel is so much better

It would be easy to regret the past
And wish we had never met
But I'm so in love with who
I am today
And the only way to get here
Was through you
And because of you
And in spite of you

I want to
Watch them grow
But keep them young
Create more memories
But slow down the clock
Give them wings
But keep them close
Parenting
Is a war against time
You never win

The happiest people I know
Are the ones that keep growing
Take the leap
Make the change
The world never stops
Moving forward
Neither should you

My heart is used
Previously broken and scarred
Banged up and patched back together again
It's not as pretty as
Some of the other hearts
You could choose

But if you want it
It's yours

If I had all the faults
You always said I did
Why doesn't he see them too?
Maybe his eyesight
Is better than yours

I don't wish you ill
Your pain won't bring me
Happiness or satisfaction
And honestly
I'm too busy chasing
My own dreams
To bother thinking
About yours
At all

I want to follow my heart
Down the rabbit hole
Of loving you
But my head warns me
That my heart was
Terrible with directions
In the past

If I never met you
Would somebody else have
Taught me what love is?
Would I think it looks different
Than I do now?
Different curves and colors and edges?
Or does love look the same to everyone
Once they find it?

Do not be defined by the
Roles you play
Yes, you are a
Daughter sister mother
Nanny maid cook
Chauffeur accountant teacher
Lover partner spouse
Employee boss middle man
But you are so much more
Than a simple noun to fill in the blank

Oh, friend
Be braver than me
Tell me the truths
That I can't see
The ones I ignore
The ones I avoid
The ones I fear
Remind me I'm strong
But imperfect
And that the biggest mistake
Is choosing ignorance
Over improvement

I was meant to find you
I don't doubt that
I just wish I knew
Whether you are a stepping-stone
Or my final destination

Is it weird that being happy
Has made me feel more confident about myself?
Or is it weirder that it took me this long
To figure out how to be happy?

I can't help but wonder
If I'd found you years ago
When we were both younger
Would I appreciate you as much
As I do now
Or would I have fucked it all up
And taken you for granted
Out of sheer ignorance

I know you're only human
And you have flaws
Just like me
But have you seen the way
Your hand fits mine?
Have you ever seen any thing
More perfect?

Love
Is the ultimate game
Of hide and seek
You have to check
All the wrong places
Before you find it
But when you do
Oh, baby, when you do
You've won the jackpot

The parts of me that
Intimidated him most
Are all the parts that
You like best

I see my boys falling in love with you
Just like I did
And it's wonderful and terrifying all at once
Because it's one thing to break my heart
But it's another thing completely to break theirs

I know there's parts of you
That you keep hidden
What I can't figure out is
Are you protecting me
Or protecting yourself

Daytime is about progress
Forward momentum and the laws of physics
Black and white and true and false
Sound logic and organized spreadsheets
Precise diction and exact numbers
Crossed off lists and followed directions
Crisp edges and perfect corners
Work and schedules and errands and the never-ending
    business of life

But the night is the opposite
The darkness is for languishing
Shades of gray and swirls of blue
Foggy reflections and damp skin
Soft words and slower touches
Long kisses and sultry gazes
Tangled limbs and sweet surrender

You can keep the day
With its frenetic energy and racing pulse
Leave me the night
With its throbbing heat and whispered confessions
Rumpled sheets and shared pillows
Shooting-star wishes and improbable dreams
I belong to the night
Because that's when you
Belong to me

I wish I could fall asleep like you
Within minutes of climbing in bed
Your mind quiet of all that keeps me awake
Instead
I overanalyze, overthink, agonize
Over problems that will still be waiting for me
In the morning
Unchanged and unsolved

Today, my kids still want to snuggle me
Want goodnight hugs and kisses
And think I have all the answers (and money)
In the world
Today, my kids cried over a videogame
And I hoped that would be the worst thing
To ever bring them tears
Today, I was the best chef in the whole wide world
When I added eggs and oil and water
To a box of cake mix
Today, water balloons were enough to make
Everything better
Today, I was a superhero when I fixed the TV
And found the missing flip flops.
Today, I was a mom
And that was enough

So many things had to fall into place
To allow us to find each other
Timing and circumstance and geography and luck
If the universe hadn't lined up just right
Would I have ever realized the tragedy of
Missing out on you?
On us?

143
You show me love
With your actions
Touch
Honesty
Attention
Time
Loyalty
And despite that
My greedy
Insecure
Romantic
Anxious
Previously broken
Heart
Sometimes
Still needs to
Hear the words too

You deserve the best
But I hope you'll accept me instead

If we ended tomorrow
I would still be grateful to you
For teaching me what love
Could look like
For teaching me what love
Should look like

I thought I'd given you my
Best years
My youth, my energy, my innocence
It's so obvious now
The best is yet to come

Stretch marks
Cellulite
Undereye circles
Scars
Gray hairs
Sagging boobs
Wrinkles
All the things I see
When I look in the mirror
But to you
I'm beautiful
Just the way I am

I could spend hours
Debating the most ridiculous things
With you
And be perfectly happy
Even if you end up being right

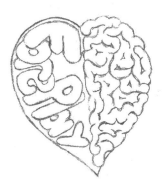

And I'm completely wrong
Because your mind
Is so damn sexy
Conversation is the
Best foreplay

There's this certain song
That reminds me of you
I hear it less and less these days
But on days when I'm missing you the most
You visit me on radio waves

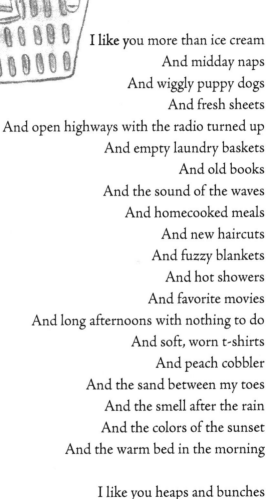

I like you more than ice cream
And midday naps
And wiggly puppy dogs
And fresh sheets
And open highways with the radio turned up
And empty laundry baskets
And old books
And the sound of the waves
And homecooked meals
And new haircuts
And fuzzy blankets
And hot showers
And favorite movies
And long afternoons with nothing to do
And soft, worn t-shirts
And peach cobbler
And the sand between my toes
And the smell after the rain
And the colors of the sunset
And the warm bed in the morning

I like you heaps and bunches

And I hope you like me too

There are women everywhere I turn
All sizes and colors and shapes
With a million different things to offer
Some days
It's hard to believe
You chose me

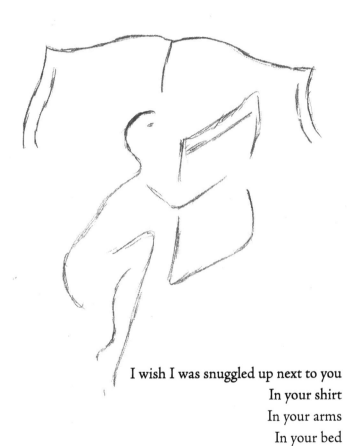

I wish I was snuggled up next to you
In your shirt
In your arms
In your bed
In your heart

One of the biggest compliments
    You've ever given me
        Without you even knowing
            Is that you feel safe enough
                To fall asleep first

This world is
Far too big
And far too beautiful
To become stagnant
Keep growing
Keep moving forward
Find your happy
It's out there
Just waiting for you

I want to stay up all night
Watch the sun
Set and rise again
So consumed by you
That sleep becomes moot

When I'm with you
It's science
Sparks
And flames
And chemistry

Don't underestimate
The healing power
Of ice cream
Puppies
Naps
Pajamas
And
Gangster rap

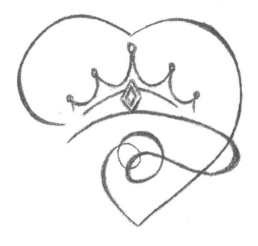

Once upon a time
The princess realized
The only thing holding her captive
Was fear and guilt
And once she let go of those
She saved herself

And became fucking awesome
And whether or not she
Found a prince
Was unimportant
Because she was born
To rule her own kingdom

Do you see
All the joy
You've added to my life?
Can you feel the
Extra happiness
That buzzes in the air
When we're together?
Even the dog can sense it
The way he wants to wiggle
In between our cuddles
Surround himself in the
Magic of us

When you're between my legs
So deep I can't keep quiet
I understand history so much better
Why wars were fought
Oceans crossed
Lands conquered
Lives altered forever
All because of the simple math
**Of two becoming one**

My favorite journey has been

From *you* and *me*

To *we*

Your actions
Day after day
Taught me what love looks like
It's the most beautiful lesson
I've ever learned

I tell you

I love you

Because with you

Holding the words in is harder

Than the fear of rejection

One day
I want to share more than
Your passenger seat
Your dessert
Your kiss
Your toothbrush
Your pillow
One day
I want to share
Your name

You were unexpected
But if I'd have known you existed
And what we would be together
I would've been
Wishing for you
On all the stars

I adore the way
You lean over and
Kiss me
When you make a sarcastic remark
So I know
You didn't mean it
Your lips tell the truth
You love me
And would
Never hurt me
On purpose

You're even better
Than the first bite of ice cream
On a summer day

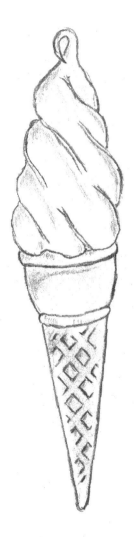

I will never get enough of your hands
Gentle enough to bring me pleasure
Strong enough to keep me safe
Big enough to hold my heart

It's funny
My kids don't carry your DNA
And yet I can see them
Learning changing growing
Because of you
And there are times

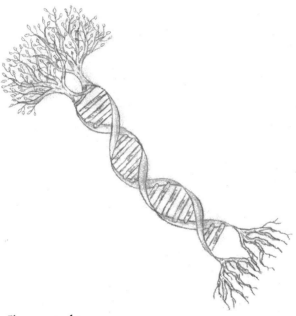

I've wanted to say
That stupid phrase
"They get it from you."
Thank you
For not letting
Silly genetics
Stop them from being yours

I could fly high before I met you
But the sky and the stars
Are far more beautiful
With you by my side

The feel of your skin
On mine
Is my worst addiction
I hope I'm never cured

If I could've seen the future
I would've still chosen to go through
All the pain in the middle
Knowing you were there at the end

Nothing feels quite as good
As your child
Asking for another hug at bedtime
Because they love you so much
And tomorrow is too far away to wait

You don't ask for anything
But my love and loyalty
Don't you see?
I would slay dragons for you

My favorite way
To fall asleep is
Stretched out next to you
Legs tangled together
Head pillowed on your shoulder
Hands entwined
Your heartbeat my lullaby

The mysterious
Alchemy of love
Is simply
Me finding you
At the right time
In the right place
Then striking a match
And watching the
Sparks ignite

I know
I have to find happiness within myself
You can't give it to me
But I would be happy
To be next to your happy
Forever

Every smile of yours
I earn
Feels like a victory

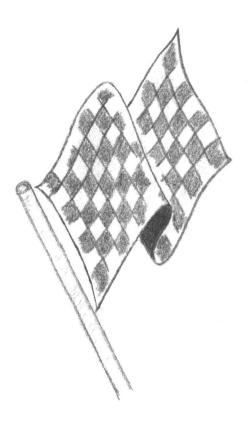

That beautiful moment
When your home
Feels like my home

When *you*
Feel like my home

I like the way I look
Through your eyes

More than what I see
In the mirror

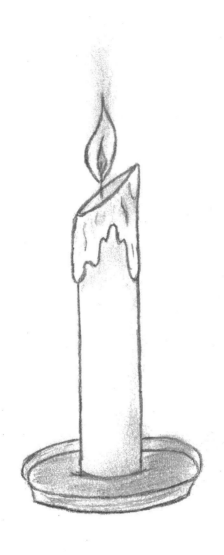

I've tossed pennies in fountains
Glimpsed shooting stars
Caught the clock at 11:11
And blown out decades worth
Of birthday candles
You're more than any wish
I've ever made

You make everything
Better
And all I want
Is to make your
Everything
Better too

The drum of my heartbeat
Keeping time with yours
The bass of your groan
Throbbing against my ear
The melody of your hips
Singing a duet with mine
I didn't know how
Sexy
**Sound was**
**Until I heard**
**The symphony of us**

I want to love you
The way you deserve
Big, bold, and
Fearless,
With infinite patience,
Sheet-scorching passion,
And a tendency to assume the best,
Not the worst,
With affection, trust,
And endless laughter,
With inside jokes,
And secret smiles,
With confidence that
I've got your back,
And the knowledge that I'll support
Your hardest decisions
And wildest dreams.
I want to love you
The way
You love me.

I have grand plans

To conquer the world

But having you next to me

Makes it an adventure

You
Tell me to soar
And ask if you can help me
**Build better wings**

# about the author

*USA TODAY* Bestseller Stacy Kestwick is a Southern girl who firmly believes mornings should be outlawed.

Her perfect day would include puppies, carbohydrates, and lounging on a hammock with a good book. No adulting, cleaning, or vegetables allowed.

## FIND ME AT:

www.stacykestwick.com

www.facebook.com/StacyKestwickAuthor

www.facebook.com/groups/StacyKestwicksTheWreck

www.stacykestwick.com/mailing-list-sign-up

www.twitter.com/stacykestwick

www.instagram.com/stacykestwick

www.goodreads.com/stacykestwick

Made in the USA
Columbia, SC
08 July 2020

13532723R00083